Oscar J:

Skipper Can No Longer Play...
and Daddy Can No Longer Stay...

Sherlene Adolphe

AuthorHouse™ UK
1663 Liberty Drive
Bloomington, IN 47403 USA
www.authorhouse.co.uk
UK TFN: 0800 0148641 (Toll Free inside the UK)
UK Local: 02036 956322 (+44 20 3695 6322 from outside the UK)

Because of the dynamic nature of the Internet, any web addresses or links contained in this book may have changed since publication and may no longer be valid. The views expressed in this work are solely those of the author and do not necessarily reflect the views of the publisher, and the publisher hereby disclaims any responsibility for them.

Any people depicted in stock imagery provided by Getty Images are models, and such images are being used for illustrative purposes only.
Certain stock imagery © Getty Images.

This book is printed on acid-free paper.

ISBN: 978-1-6655-9357-1 (sc)
ISBN: 978-1-6655-9356-4 (e)

Library of Congress Control Number: 2021919772

Print information available on the last page.

Published by AuthorHouse 10/08/2021

authorHOUSE

Skipper & OscarJ

For as long as he could remember,
Oscar J had his bouncy dog Skipper with him every day.

For as long as he could remember,
Oscar J and his bouncy dog Skipper would go out to play.

Skipper?

Well he was a great big dog,
Black and tan,
With huge big paws the size of a grown man's hands.

He'd wag his long tail,
And pant and bark,
As he'd run through the house,
And play fetch in the park.

Every birthday of Oscar's Skipper was there,
Bounding among the presents,
Playing musical chairs,

Spring chasing bunnies through the meadow,
Summer catching frisbee by the sea,
Autumn running through the bracken,
Christmas lounging beside the tree,

For as long as he could remember...

Throughout his nursery, infants, and junior school years,
At the end of each long day,
Oscar would return home to find Skip by the front door,
Eagerly waiting to go out and play.

Then the time came when Skipper could no longer jump as high,
Or even run very fast.
In any race with Oscar Skip would be guaranteed first place,
But now he would always come last.

With each passing year Skip's coat would pepper with grey,
Jet black whiskers began to turn white,
Pain developed in his joints causing a slight limp,
Followed by some gradual loss of his sight.

"It's all due to old age" said the Vet,
"These are problems we would expect,
all I can do is prescribe some relief for the pain,
the rest we must accept."

Where Skipper would have preferred to run he could now only walk,
Where he would have preferred to stand he would now sit or lay,
Although he'd still eagerly await Oscar's return home from school,
Skip would now be too tired to play.

So Oscar would sit with his furry friend,
To scratch behind his ears, beneath his chin, stroke his tum.
Being fed any treats Oscar found in the cupboard after school,
So they could still enjoy time with one another and have fun.

Then one day Oscar returned home to find Skip wasn't there.
Not hiding behind any door that he searched or beneath any chair.

When Oscar called out for Skipper he just didn't come,
Confused – Oscar went in search of his mum.

"Oh Oscar dear I didn't hear you come in."

"Hi – Mum" he then asked; "where's Skip?"

"I have some very sad news I'm afraid, so please come and take a seat.
As you know Skip was of a grand old age, not as fit as he used to be.
He had awful pain in his joints, was deaf in one ear and at the end he could hardly see."

"The end"

"Well my son, it all became too much, and now dear Skip is no more, when I arrived from shopping earlier today he was found laying quite dead by the door."

"Dead?"

"Yes – I'm ever so sorry he's gone."
"Was it my fault? what did I do?
Did he go because I behaved badly the other day and refused to listen to you?"

"No!"

"Well if I'm especially good will he come back?
I promise to now always listen,
eat my greens, and never again torment our new neighbours cat!"

"Dear Oscar,
now that our lovely Skipper has now died;
he can no longer move,
no longer hear,
no longer see.

so never again will he be able to come running to either you, daddy or me.

Try to imagine Skip's death as though he's in a very, very, deep sleep.
Never to awake from the 'Land of Nod' counting up all those sheep."

As hard as he tried Oscar J couldn't imagine a life without Skip,
For each part of his life that he could recall Skip had always been in it.

For as long as he could remember...

With a huge ache in his heart, and a pounding head,
Eyes over flowing with tears Oscar took to his bed.

Staring out through his bedroom window, up at the cloudy sky.
Tears rolling down his cheeks Oscar turned to ask his mum; "why?"

She replied;

"Just as each year green leaves brown falling dead from a tree,
all that is now living one day may die,
and those like us that have lost one that they love,
may feel the sadness of such a loss and may cry."

"Its not fair!" Oscar shouted,
"Why do our new neighbours still have their cat?
why didn't Julie's two guinea pigs lay down and die?
or even Daniel's ugly pet rat?"

"Honey this is something called grief that you are feeling,
that only time will heal.
But with each good memory that you can muster, the less anger and pain you will feel."

"Good memories? What if I can't remember? what if I forget?"

And with that Oscar's mother embraced him tightly as he wept.

She soothed...

"Honey we have all his belongings;
film and photographs taken throughout the years,
we can put them somewhere special as keepsake,
and perhaps wipe away some of these tears."

"What if the films get broken or ruined?
Photo's are good but not the same.
I can't believe die and dead has made my best friend disappear,
never to be seen again."

"Over time his belongings may become broken, ruined, or lost – the
list can even extend.
But keepsakes are not the only way for you to remember your dear
friend.
There maybe time when the hurt seems too much,
as Skip is already so dearly missed.
Remember the pain of your grief wont always be so bad, especially
when you remember to do this...

Close your eyes Oscar,
shut them real tight,
now try to imagine Skipper with all your might."

"Why?"

"Try to imagine the sound of his bark,
the feel of his hair..."

"It's fur mum"

"Okay! But do you see him there?"

"Umm? Yes I can see him;
Chasing his ball through the park.
Wagging his tail by the front door.
Trying to bury a bone out back.
Now he's rolling around on the floor..."

Now I can hear him!
Snoring at night,
barking when the postman delivers our mail,"

Oscar giggled,

"I can see him begging for scraps in the kitchen
And now he's chasing his tail!"

Oscars eyes slowly opened.

"Wow mum thats amazing!
I understand now!
Now I can see!
That even though Skip has gone from our lives, there's a way I can keep him with me!"

Although the ones we have loved and lost can never return to us once they have gone,
As long as their memories remain in our hearts and in our minds their spirit will forever live on.

For as long as we can remember...

"Oh just shut up! Just get out!"

Shouted Oscar's mum from the hallway below,
"Why don't you just get out of my hair,
pack up your things and go?"

"You wish it was so simple!" shouted back his Dad,
"You must be crazy to think I'd just walk away from all I've ever had!"

Oscar J let out a sob and pulled his duvet over his head,
Sending out a silent prayer that it would muffle anymore that they said.

Tomorrow was the class spelling test,
With so many words for him to recite,
But he couldn't ask mum or dad to help him revise whilst they were
in the middle of a fight...

These constant rows had been happening for so many weeks they
seemed like years,

Always involving harsh words, slammed doors and many many tears.

Romantic meals and dinner dances used to be their quality time alone,
When Oscar would get spoilt over at Nanny and Gramps,
Or have fun with the sitter at home.

To the fairground,
Barbeque's,
Swimming and to the park,
They went as a family,
And sometimes invited Ronnie and his parents from No. 23.

Oscar would think back to those times,
When his parents would hug, kiss and have fun.
Those were of the good old days when Oscar's dad was besotted with his mum.

Now he'd always find mum tearful,
In her bedroom on the phone,
Telling friends and family what else had gone wrong at home.

Dad?

He may not now be seen for many days on end,
Should he ask mum of dad's whereabouts,
He was always away on business or staying with a friend.

Dinner at home was no longer as fresh and fancy as it used to be; mainly frozen meals, takeaways or pies donated from No. 23.

When Aunty Pearl came to visit she told Oscar's mum;
"Sis, you look a state!"
It was due to mums puffy eyes from all of her crying,
and loosing too much weight.

Aunty Pearl advised mum to be honest with young Oscar,
and no longer pretend.
So that she and Mr J could make a final decision,
Bringing this awful situation to an end...

✓✓✓✓✓✓✓

The kids hurried out as at 10:30hrs the bell went to single first play,
Mr Hall approached Oscar who for past weeks was unusually last to leave,
And asked him to wait as he had something to say...

"Oscar J I have to ask what has got into you?
You used to be a fine captain of your team and perfect prefect at this school.
Now you're always late to class,
your attendance has become poor,
your A/B grades are failing – something that's never happened before.

Do you want to tell me about why you think this is?
It's not just me that's noticed a change,
But also your friends, and some of the other kids."

"Why don't they mind their own business!?" shouted Oscar,
"What's it got to do with them? I bet I know who grassed me up,
and they try to say that they're my friends!"

Oscar looked down at his boots – he had nothing else to say,
He'd find out who grassed him up to Mr Hall and they were going
to pay.

Feeling two hands on his shoulders,
Oscar looked up,
Mr Hall's eyes were now level with his own,
"Oscar" his tutor asked gently,
"Is everything okay at home?"

Hot tears stung the back of Oscar's eyes but now he didn't care,
It was then his legs seemed to give way and he sunk into a chair,

Mr Hall grabbed a box of tissues from his desk...

~~~~~~~

"What's it like not to have a dad?" asked Ronnie,
"Yeah," said Susie "is Mr J's leaving true?"
"Actually I heard it was Oscar's ma that got booted out." chuckled
Aaron,
"I wonder what she was up to?"

"What are you lot saying about my parents?" shouted Oscar approaching,
"Aaron how dare you disrespect my mum! You want a reason to gossip about me and mine? Come here you're gonna get one!"

Seeing red Oscar swung a punch which would have hit Aaron square on the chin,
If it wasn't for caretaker Mr Dempsey passing and quickly jumping in-between...

"Sorry sir" Oscar mumbled for the thump he'd now given Mr Dempsey's chest,
"It's time you followed me to your Head Teacher's office and laid that fist down for a bit of rest."

Oscar let the school care taker lead the way.

"Mrs J before you leave the grounds may I have a word?
I have some bad news about Oscar in a fight earlier I'm afraid"

"A fight?"

"I know,
for him it seems completely absurd."

While Oscar was directed to one of the homework groups in the lower school gym,
Mr Hall proceeded with his mum back to his class where they would both discuss him within.

Oscar hung his head in shame,
Staring at the wooden gym floor,

He couldn't understand why he kept behaving so bad,
He'd never been this way before.

~~~~~~~~

Mrs J stared in disbelief,
As she had no idea,
That the problems of the past four or five months,
Had caused Oscar so much despair...

Okay he'd wet the bed a few times,
and on weekends he no longer went out to play,
But she'd thought this was a pre-teen phase that would simply go away.
Sitting there with Mr Hall at 10 minutes to four,
It dawned on Mrs J this supposed phase had been caused by so very much more...

Mrs J apologised to Mr Hall,
For although ashamed and embarrassed she did accept,
His observations and concerns regarding his 'home life' theory about her son,
As being totally correct.

When she went to collect Oscar from his group in the lower school gym,
She vowed never again to loose sight of the most important person of all – him...

~~~~~~~~~

"Once upon a time dad and I were so very happy,
sadly that has now changed.
Although we still care deeply for one another,
our lives are no longer the same.

That is why we have decided to divorce;
to part,
to lead our own separate lives.
It's not what either of us ever wanted but staying together has already been tried."

"Is this my fault?" cried Oscar, "What did or didn't I do?"
"Son." Answered Mr J, "this has absolutely nothing to do with you.
It's due to my differences with mummy and you're certainly not to blame.
But as so many youngsters feel they may be the reason for their parents breaking up,

so I understand why you may feel the same.
No, son the fault is not your own."

Mrs J took her Oscar's hand.

"The heartache of this break-up is affecting us all honey.
Especially poor you.
But for you to avoid experiencing any of our pain is what we had
hoped to do.

Oscar dear from our hearts please accept this apology,
For the pain and disruption caused to your life by your daddy and
by me."

Oscar nodded his head then asked;

"Mummy now that daddy is going,
does it mean you will go too?
If I don't have a mum or dad then what will I do?

As I'm not near old enough to try and live alone,
will I get taken by the Social and put into a home?"

"Goodness no!" said his Dad,
"You'll have two homes - just wait and see!
One right here with mummy,
and one home away with me.

Christmas and Birthdays will be as special as before.
But now you'll get **not one but two sets of presents!**
So you can look forward to more!"

"So," asked Oscar, "does this mean you both still love me and want me as your son?"

"Oscar my champ" replied Mr J "that fact has never been in question!
One thing you can be sure of is that on the day of your birth,
was the day your mother and I became the proudest parents on earth!"

Sadly in life there may come a time when two parents decide on separation.

Although a huge change, certain to remain for their daughters and sons is their constant love and adoration!

About the Author

Born in London England on 6th January 1980, Sherlene Adolphe was raised in Southfields Wimbledon, a London Borough of the same.

Her love for poetry developed from a very early age, and was a regular pastime much to the benefit of her family and friends!

Qualified at Carshalton College in the London Borough of Sutton, Sherlene pursued a successful career in Business Travel, moving on into Lettings and Property Management, all of which she thoroughly enjoyed and excelled.

From the age of twenty one, alongside her formal careers, it was Sherlene's work among children and adolescents within the Social Care sector, that provided her with a great basis of her knowledge and experience of the same. Also registered Foster Carer, Sherlene currently lives in Beddington village. A tiny rural suburb in Surrey Greater London, with Omar her son and only child.

Printed in the United States
by Baker & Taylor Publisher Services